Peter's Easter Story

The story of Peter receiving forgiveness from the risen Savior

Luke 5:1–11, 12:12; Matthew 16:13–20,
26:31–46, 69–75; John 21:15–19

Written by Nicole E. Dreyer
Illustrated by Keiko Motoyama

Arch® Books
Copyright © 2004 Concordia Publishing House
3558 S. Jefferson Avenue, St. Louis, MO 63118-3968
Manufactured in Colombia

Simon was a fisherman;
He sailed with James and John.
His brother Andrew fished with them,
They worked from dusk 'til dawn.

One bright morning Jesus came
And called the men to shore.
They raised their nets at His command,
And they could hold no more.

Then Simon bowed before the Lord,
"I am a sinful man."
But Jesus smiled and shook His head,
"From now on you'll catch men!"

Simon heard the Master's words
And left his boat on shore.
He went with Andrew, James, and John,
To follow Christ the Lord.

Jesus knew that one day soon
This man would lead His flock.
Then Jesus changed this
        disciple's name
To Cephas—Peter—"Rock."

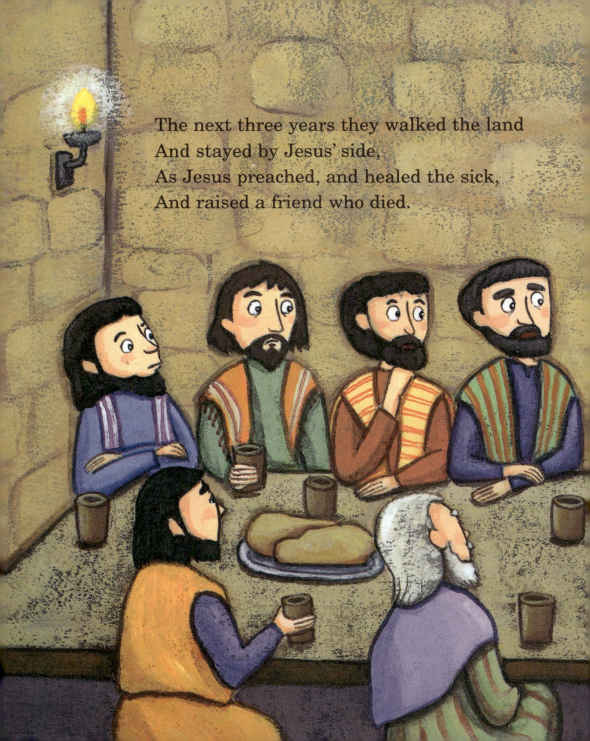

The next three years they walked the land
And stayed by Jesus' side,
As Jesus preached, and healed the sick,
And raised a friend who died.

At Passover, the Lord's last meal,
They gathered to eat, then pray.
But Jesus knew they soon would run,
'Though Peter swore he'd stay.

"Peter," Jesus said to him,
"Before the rooster crows
Three times from Me you'll turn away;
You'll deny it's I you know."

In the garden late that night
Soldiers took Jesus away.
Peter followed close behind
To hear what Pilate would say.

But in the courtyard, as he watched,
Peter chose to lie:
"I do not know Him," he said three times,
Then ran away and cried.

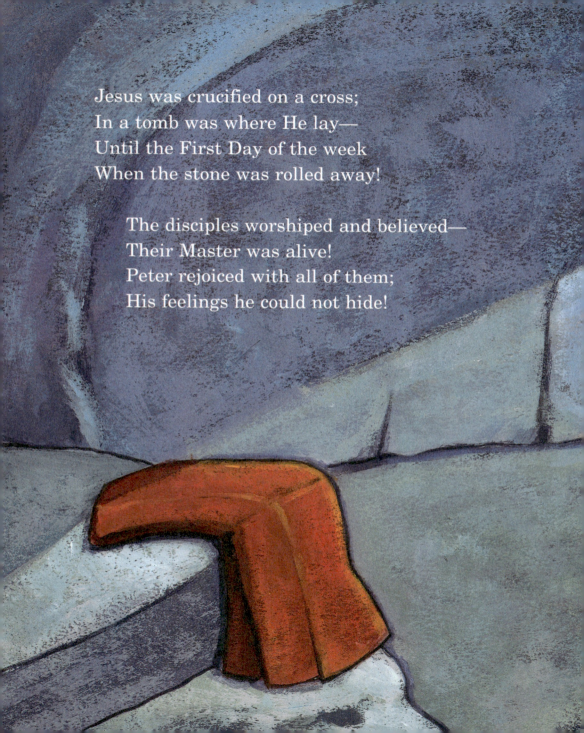

Jesus was crucified on a cross;
In a tomb was where He lay—
Until the First Day of the week
When the stone was rolled away!

The disciples worshiped and believed—
Their Master was alive!
Peter rejoiced with all of them;
His feelings he could not hide!

Again one morning Jesus came
And stood beside the sea.
He took from Pete the fish they'd caught;
"Come eat and talk with Me."

"Do you love Me?" Jesus asked.
"My Lord, You know I do!"
"Then, feed My lambs," our Lord declared,
"That's what I ask of you."

Jesus asked him this three times;
Peter's answer for all three:
"Yes, I love You, Lord," he said.
Then Christ said, "Follow Me!"

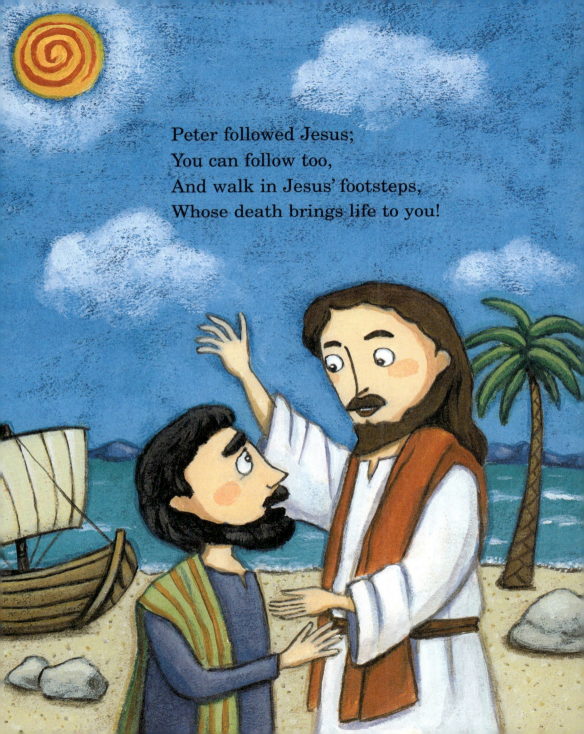

Peter followed Jesus;
You can follow too,
And walk in Jesus' footsteps,
Whose death brings life to you!

Dear Parents,

Jesus called Peter "the Rock" because he confessed that Jesus was the Christ who was to come into the world. This confession of the Christian teachings by Peter is the foundation of the Christian church (Matthew 16:18). At the time of Jesus' crucifixion, though, Peter was not so strong. He was still a sinner. When he was confronted with the harsh reality of living as one of Jesus' followers, he quickly turned his back on his Savior and Master. Peter may have felt that his own life was at stake—so he lied to protect himself.

How could Peter, who had been with Jesus for years and heard the true teachings about the Christ, turn away? On his own, Peter did not have the strength to stand firm in his faith. And on his own, Peter could do nothing to earn forgiveness. Grief-stricken, guilt-ridden, a repentant Peter at last understood that Jesus was the true Savior of the world.

Faith in the grace and forgiveness that comes only through Christ the Lord is a gift. Peter received it through no merit of his own. It comes to us the same way. When we are baptized, we receive this gift of faith. When we hear God's Word and partake of the Lord's Supper, this faith is refreshed and forgiveness is imparted. Like Peter, we are in the presence of the resurrected Jesus.

Use this Easter story to teach your child that the world still confronts us about our association with Jesus. Every time we are asked to answer for our faith, we go through an experience similar to Peter's. And just like the risen Savior strengthened and forgave Peter, He gives us strength and forgiveness too!

The Editor